ISBN: 9798606200603

also by alannah radburn:

Yellow (2017)

excerpts from my exorcism (2018)

from 'the nature of love' trilogy:

on a cherry perfect eve (2019)

instagram: @alannahradburn.poetry

foreword:

Alannah and I stumbled upon each other and I've always felt like it was true serendipity at work. Our poetry has always had a way of fitting together without us knowing or trying. I planned a clementine-themed release and Alannah published "on a cherry perfect eve." Now I have the honor of introducing her lilac child and you can probably guess the color of my next release, which happens to have a floral theme as well. Some people get competitive, but not Alannah and I. We lift each other up, empower each other, and embrace these beautiful coincidences. It's something to celebrate when you find another human that speaks the words of your heart. Why shy away from a soul like that when you can hold their hand and walk through the field of lilacs together?

The universe brought this talented soul into my life and I'm forever grateful. There are times when even poets, people sewn together by words and emotion, can't get their pen to say the things their heart is screaming. Several times while reading "on a lilac laced dusk" I had to stop because Alannah just knew. She knew the words I felt but couldn't say. She took feelings I had buried and breathed life into them; held out her hand as they climbed out of their grave.

One of my favorite poets, Alannah Radburn, wrote "in matters of love and war, you'll find me unearthing landmines and planting flowers in their place." I've been through both love and war and fallen on my fair share of landmines, but I know a planted flower when I see one. I'm both honored and over the moon to present to you "on a lilac laced dusk."

-- Jessyca

table of contents

for my family

i welcome you to spread your frail lies
about me like hot whispers through a megaphone:
tell your friends, tell the town, tell the world,
tell him.
my story, my life, my truth is mine,
and i have the ability to write it.
you've always been a gifted storyteller,

but i've always been better.

violet nightmare

heartbreak is a hitman
and there is a colossal bounty on my head.
the most chilling thing about heartbreak is that

she is a remorseless hunter;
she never brings me back alive.

run for your life

my mind has tripled in weight with grief,
my neck may snap under the added pressure,
my head may simply roll away.

should you come across it,
you'd likely kick it aside,
like school children walking home might do with a
pebble,
a pinecone,
an icicle,
or some other object of insignificance.

    dead weight

my home became salem in 1692;
i, the witch.
one night they set my room on fire as warning,
but it was morning when the apocalypse came.
the next time i walked through the entryway,
i found a stake driven into the ground.
there was plenty of rope;
matches littered the floor.
the woman i lived with had slid them into my hair
like bobby pins.
i knew her to be superstitious, but not like this.
she grated my head against the doorway, rough.
enough to ignite the flame.
i called to her with love,
and she answered in fire.
what happened in the home that day rendered it to
ruin:
hate can masterfully craft destruction with the right
fuel.
she may think she is rid of me, but her own hand
ensures my immortality.
the smell of smoke clings to her clothes,
to her hair.

it reminds her exclusively of me.

    a parting gift

you sucked the wind right out of my sails,
took a machete to their canvas,
snapped the mast for good measure.

chummed the water and threw me to the sharks

just to be sure.

he empties out a drawer,
tells me to fill it with my things.
says that this is where i live now.
i spend the whole day unpacking,
and i make it perfect. just so.

the next morning he tells me
he's changed his mind;
we cannot live together.
i spend the whole day packing.
and i leave it perfect. just so.

he doesn't say goodbye.

one of us is homeless, one of us is heartless

how to fall out of love with someone who no longer loves you

- go camping by the ocean with your family. get rained on and bitten by mosquitos. let your older brother annoy you, and stay up late staring into the fire.

- listen to amy shark with your best friend. climb mountains with her when you're hungover. sweat, and despite it all, laugh.

- sit across from your two grandmothers. soak in their wisdom. respect their matriarchy. believe them when they tell you *he ain't shit*.

- build rubik's-cube vexing ikea furniture with your younger cousin. help organize her new apartment with her not new boyfriend. take solace in her happiness.

- know that one day, this happiness will come back to you in spades.

believe me

it disturbs me still
to think of how much i compromised for her
when she remained rigid--
an unmoving thing.
never once compromising for me.
what is a relationship? i ask myself.
not this. never this.

the steel must be warmed,
softened
before the blacksmith can create new,
beautiful craftsmanship.

she was frigid from the day i met her.

this is the poem.
the one to remind you
that sadness is a normal human emotion.

it does not always mean that the depression is back.

it is not always the monster rearing its head once
more.

you are free to feel

the rug has not been pulled,
it has been violently dismantled,
torn to pieces underfoot:
uncovering dark information is a bloodsport.
as the common tale goes, there is a person i thought i
knew.

i wish i could scour back through the books i've
written,
tear out every page about her.
light them on fire,
send the ashes back to her bed,
back to the smouldering pile of deception on which
she dreams up mundane ways to interfere in the
business of others.
(there is nothing creative about sharing private
conversations).

the books are published, the poems cannot be
unwritten--
but this one will give them new life;
will tilt them to expose the vicious, seething
underbelly that was always there.

some people are so selfish, they see the world
not through rose coloured glasses,
but through a lens that reflects only themselves in
everything they see.
they choose to meddle in affairs that have nothing to
do with them
as their spite is hungrier than their spirit.

as for you,
you've always had endless conversation
about experiences that were never yours.
tinkering with the lives of others
does not excuse not knowing how to live your own.

i will never write of you again,
but consider this a parting gift.
i'd say see you in hell,
but only the most exalted villains make it that far, and
you

you have no honour.

j

i used to write of your ocean hands as something
that could turn the sharpest parts of me soft;
just like seaglass.
now i know that they are only capable
of drowning everyone in their wake.

poseidon's slave

he had no problem accepting my divinity when it
served him.
but as soon as the wind picked up,
and whispers of a great wildfire reached our home,
        he did not support me.
rather, he watched wordlessly as they crucified me
with a stake through my chest.
        he even hammered it once or twice.
call me vampire,
call me witch,
call me scarecrow;
the woman who hung in front of the town,
warning others to stay far,
far from this place.

        omen

she threatened to steal my art,
but you can't burn the bridges of songs,
the lyrics of my poems.
sure, you can refuse to return my poetry books
but damn,
you can't change how i make people feel.

nice try

what is more holy than a woman with nothing to lose?

you wish to rid your world of me
but i'm already a wraith;
    travel by wind,
slip through your fingers.
sure, keep reaching back to your quiver, bow in
hand--
you're grasping at air (grasping at straws).
could your arrow disable the clouds in the sky,
     or are you irrelevant?
look to the heavens and pray,
for you have no more ammunition.
i grin with blood-stained teeth
and ribs splintered through skin,
          do your worst:

     it means absolutely nothing.

there's a saying that my therapist has been sharing
with me for years.
recently, my mom has started to say it too,
as well as a favourite singer of mine.
in simpler words,
the universe is trying to funnel this directly into my
brainstem:

the opposite of love is not hate,

it is indifference.

and so,

this autumn, may each leaf upon which you step be
not limp and wet,
but not make a satisfactory crunch either.
may your soy milk coffee be lukewarm,
with no sweetness of cinnamon within.

may you be as bored as you are boring.

for the first time since you did what you did,
i do not hate you.

and, whoever you are,

   that is so much worse.

my goddess,
no wonder i feel so much.
the universe is ever expanding,
something must now fill all that extra space between
the stars.

 emotions

it was like a circus act:
how far you bent over backwards
to ensure my misery.

contortionist

patterns just may be the most natural thing on the
planet;
we find the fibonacci sequence in the seed spirals of
sunflowers,
in the shell of a mollusk.
the orb spider creates a near perfectly circular web,
and bees produce stunning symmetry in their
honeycombs.
the rings of the trees look the same
as the prints of our fingers.
there are patterns in pythagorean triples,
in frosty snowflakes.
many minds throughout history
have found these perfections to exist in the natural
world.

when we tried to change some of our patterns
to something healthier--
better,
it seemed that this time nature conspired to disallow
it.
everything was already written,
and it wasn't in the stars.

so we fell from our perfect symmetry,

        into disarray.

stir the tea
in counter clockwise fashion.
the small silver spoon chimes elegantly against the
china:
the soft clinking of your exile;

the sweet bell of your banishment.

darling,
they tried to make a monster of our love.
they said it was a vile thing, plucked fresh from the
swamp,
writhing with leeches.
they took our affection and painted it the deepest
colours
of their judgement.
didn't let it dry before throwing ash and dirt,
willing it to stick,
praying that we couldn't breathe underneath.
they went around telling everyone that our
relationship
was damning the town,
corrupting the water supply,
that we needed to be killed
lest we kill them.
darling, they tried to make a monster of our love,
and one fateful dawn
they broke the locks on your doors,
got inside. made you believe it too.
my sweet baby,

they made you believe it too.

move on.
he makes it sound easy,
the words drift from his mouth
as if they aren't softly floating towards a raging
waterfall.
the phrase batters me, like it's my fault that i loved
him more,
but i swear to you the only fault of mine runs between
the tectonics
of what i want and what i know i deserve;
this is when the quake happens.
my hands start to shake,
and soon the whole world will be imploding
if i remain stagnant.

and so i move

    on.

there were five women:
self proclaimed champions of other women--
let me restart.

there were five lying women.

they took the five beautiful points of our pentacle
and flipped it upside down--
made it evil.

tried to rip the spirit from my circle
using the most vicious of spells.

they do not understand magic
and cannot comprehend that their
acid-laced words won't pierce my protection.

it only showed me what they really are:

hags.

as we hugged goodbye,
you stealthily slid a blade into my lower back,
came back seven months later to twist it,
tear it out,
brandish it like some gruesome kebab
of intestines and organs.
and that is fine,
because this is my poem,
my metaphor.

you, however,
have to live in the crushing
daily reality
of being a bad person.

i get to live with love

it isn't always a loud,
howling thing
when they come for you--
leeches don't have fangs,
you can't feel them attach,

but they'll suck your veins dry regardless.

as a girl, i thought myself a magnificent dragon.
strong. soaring;
mythical.

as you grow, others impose upon your girlhood;
show you the ugly inside them.

well, i was finally a dragon.
but then they peeled back my outsides,
        scale by scale.

until i was left bare skinned,
with not a lick of fire left in my body.

truth as an unruly sword

chariots scream across the sky
pulled by flaming hooves.
dark raindrops lash my cheeks
joining torrents of salt water.

nothing will grow from this rain.
it pounds my fool's paradise
back under the soggy dirt;

where all good things go to die.

after you both, i was sucked so very dry.
parched of everything i had to give.
i'd never been so thirsty.
your rivers were overflowing,
thousands of droplets wrung from my compassion.

for weeks i couldn't get close to a flame--
i'd take to it like tissue paper.

could sit in a sauna for days without
shedding a drop.
couldn't afford a single tear to fall.

hibernation. rehydration.
give everything i have

to myself for a change.

the rains have come and
not a drop has fallen into your well.
this is what it means to plant roots

and water them.

     drink up

a party,
in my name!
an altar of indecency
built by many hands--
to honour me.
you've brought together all of your hags
to revel in the horror of my very existence.
you have an utterly bizarre way of showing how
much you hate me,
dear.
it looks an awful lot more
like desperate
obsession
to me.

gorgon's toast

hottest summer on record. even the mayflowers are
dying.
coldest winter yet. brutal. heard the
neighbour's fingers froze right off.

every winter. every summer.
it's the same story, the same tales.
the same is true for heartbreak:
the most recent is always the worst.
but you've survived every single year until now.
sweet one,

you will be around to complain of the heat next year.

forecast

they turned the dull, metallic taste of blood
into something shimmering
and kind.
my dear alchemists,
thank you.

family

how do you write words detailing the loss of a child?
for the poets' words are meant to be easy. but this
time. words are unable to access the pain. it's too
deep. i can't equalize the pressure--
i can't go that far down…

to describe what it's like. do i want to?
i spent every day and every night with him. he slept in
my room.
his breathing; a soft lullaby that tucked me in during
the moonrise. our adventures belonged to no one but
us.

my sweet little one. this is my lullaby to you.

you taught me the magic of empathy. the enchantment
of unconditional. the finality of

    goodbye.

at first i was wave after wave of melancholy.
all sappy anguish,
crashing onto the steady shores of my family.
then some time went by and i realized how
much more of it i had.
i'm not tied to your every move,
not at the whim of your ever changing schedule--
not under your control.

prying the weight of your heavy thumb
off of my back
has left me all muscle,

    no weight.

i will never stop curating the love that i want.
i will waltz through the judgement of others
like lilac fields at night.

like the air is always warm and scented

sickly sweet

i know of a great goddess;
a creator.
when the rivers of my sadness come,
she whispers to me that i need not hold back my tears,
she holds them for me.
cupped in her kind hands,
she waters meadows and reminds me
that how i feel is a gift of life.
that everything grows because of me.
some call her queen, some call her empress,
some call her by the sound of her compassion.
all i know is she needs not a crown--
her presence is enough;
commanding, passionate, loyal
the words start to weave around her delicious mind
until they form a coronation in their own right.
the flowers bloom in ecstasy.
we laugh until the earth glows in time with
our own beating hearts.

best friend

this scarlet ache turns pale under your hand:
like i've never kissed a burn.
like this skin has never been blistered.

salve-ation

i wrung out my spine
like a used washcloth.
it rained and rained,
and a full forest tumbled out;
    but it was all wrong.
the pine needles changed and fell,
painting the ground a crimson carpet.
the conifers lost the greens of forever
and burned alive in the autumn.
i am a volatile being with no permanence,
but i can guarantee

    one hellfire of a show.

would you like some tea with your summer?
lounge in the shady spot
of the august backyard.

pour it over ice baby,
        keep it nice and cold.

   vegas

watching you bite that apple is something of an
experience, love.
the sweetness spills over,
and suddenly the birds are all singing your name,
landing upon me like snow white.
the sun shines her honeyed hello,
and all at once we are speaking the language of
dandelions;
wishing,
  wishing

     for this moment to stay.

the resilience of women will always be passed
from one to the other

in whispered verse,
through underground tunnels,
pressed between the pages of a hardcover book;

whether it be in secret,
    or
from the ashes of one to the blood of another,

our way will always be found.

after margaret atwood

if you are sailing in my sea,
        i can promise you this:
ample wind,
plenty of water,

sparsely salted;

        just enough to keep it interesting.

is there an ounce of tenderness left
under your scales;
is there a single shred of sensibility
rooted in my cloven hooves?

we have turned each other
into depictions of the devil.

why did you betray me?

there was a time when we drank red wine from the
same bottle
watched our favourite show from the same screen
...slept in the same bed.

the first night your casper mattress arrived
i shared it with you. there is not a night you sleep on
it
that exists without me having pre dated that space
on that mattress
during your slumber.

that must count for something right?

    it doesn't

you have spent nights gazing at the stars in
wonderment,
feeling out how you fit into this immensity.
in a world already so infinite,
you have no use for a person who will make you feel
even more insignificant.

send them out to sea;

ask them if they now know the meaning of feeling
small.

immensity

i wish i could have been more than a stepping stone
on your path to self discovery;
i wish i could have been more than just a portrait on
the wall.
when you get to where you're going, swift-stepper,
i hope you'll remember how soft i was underfoot
when your feet needed resting for a moment.

i hope that the air was clear;

i hope that your heart was full.

i was strong in the knees before i met you.

you had me in the palm of your hand,
until i dove into your creased fate line,
rode it like a current right out of there.

this is not beyond my control

the day you told me that you needed space and time
as if this were some kind of continuum,
as if this could ever continue,
as if there was any more endurance to this love,
as if we hadn't already run a marathon a day for the
last three days straight,
i took out a restraining order against my depression.
yes,
i was losing the man.
i was losing the kid.
i was losing my home, my job, my city.
this did not mean that i was losing the hot, roiling
core in my center.
and yes, my brain wanted to jump right back on
to those nicely dug out railroad tracks that the
depression had carved
years earlier at the hands of another man.
but damn
had it ever taken a lot of years and a lot of therapy to
grow some foliage around those tracks,
to let nature reclaim them,
to disallow the neurons from creating the bullet train
they ever so desired
          because that would be easy.
not today, depression.
so,
off we went to court,
this roiling core in my centre and the rest of me that
was left,
          the autopilot that refused to let the plane go
down—

this should be the proudest day of my therapist's life.

i dug out my scythe, and i looked like death.

but i swung hard,
i mowed a new path through the tall grass, a new
track for the neurons.
more of a gentle walkway than a bullet train.
there is space to cultivate along the way,
to enjoy the views here.
this passage is no shortcut,
but it can only end in rebuilding the body around this

*hot
roiling
core.*

every time i try to drown myself,
the other half of me grabs my neck,
pries my mouth open
and forces the air in.
tells me my lungs are too loud to be muted by water.
it's not pretty,
but it's survival.
it's not perfect,
but some days it's the only form of breath there is.

a girl's gills

at this time last year
she was in love with me;
so wildly that the tulips on the table were opening so
wide,
reaching for so much,
so drunk on the air of our desire
that their petals inverted and drifted to the wood
below.

this year, no one is in love with me,
yet i saw a tulip greet me with such reverence
its petals flipped and peeled back the first layer of
stem.
the air still dances when i speak.

love has nothing to do with her

when you are at the end of your rope,
i will knot mine to it
and keep you going.
when i am at the end of my rope,
you tie the beginning of yours
to my end.

this is how we are never alone:
if you should find yourself lost,
put your hand to the rope;

    it will circle you right back to me.

aphrodite lay with venus

*and discovered that it was herself she loved
all along.*

when the lilacs first emerged this year,
i feared that i was doomed.
every time i took in their sweetness,
i expected to hear your voice in my mind,
reminding me that it's your favourite smell,
favourite flower.
instead,
when i smell the lilacs,
heavy in the air at dusk,
i see my childhood home.
my mother is in the driveway,
crooning to her small daughter.
sharing her love of the scent.
some memories are more foundational than others.
some people give their love,

and never take it away.

moments pass.
what was, was.
it's all the organic movement of things.
it's all healing,
and strife,
and wind.
let it be everything. let it be momentary.

let it be nothing at all.

the day your honesty fell from the sky,
landing on me like a grand piano,
i plucked the eyelashes from my face one by one;
made 200 wishes and tossed them to the wind.
with nothing left to catch them,
i made a tincture of my tears,
used it to season my cocktails
with just the correct amount of bitterness.
rose petals simmer on the stove;
there are so many jars lined up on the window ledge,
i don't know which heals what anymore.

is there a cure for honesty?
i ask the sea,
and all she does is invite me to walk in,
up to my ears,
hear her roar

    and remind myself that i can do the same.

should this lilac love ever die

i'll lift the veil,
as if our wedding day,
and cross to the other side.

here,
we will meet
and kiss the flower petals

in everlasting afterlove.

purple poison

it was the cusp of autumn,
and
knowing my great devotion to the romance
of an old train,
of misted lamp lights and whispering winds,
my great love took us down to the old track;
polaroid camera and picnic basket in hand.
but sweet goddess, we did not walk hand in hand
under the tangerine late summer's moon.
the only blaring light bestowed upon us
was the headlights of the steam engine
barreling through a cold haze.

snake charmer, necromancer,
he raised a rope from the basket
and tied our relationship to the tracks
with the most complicated of knots.

watching the train dismember every limb of our love
was
like sliding a small straw into my lungs
and slowly,
slowly
extracting every breath i've ever taken.
draining, siphoning my lifeblood.
he took it all
gathered it into a locket that he wears so piously
around his neck.

serial killers always keep a trophy.

i am covered in your fingerprints.

i am the scene of a crime.

my home became salem in 1692;
i, the witch.
they threw around words like
'hysteria' and 'vile',
heaved them at me like stones.
they strapped my wrists and ankles to a heavy oak
chair,
threw me in the river.
she'll float, the witch will float
they chant to the currents.

    i never surfaced for air.

    persecution

i have experienced the absolute worst this world has
to offer
because i've had the best that there is.

losing him

it is a fearsome, gruesome thing
when a heart is split so wide sky open.
tissue and muscle ripped in all directions;
the mouth of a kraken,
a supernova of grief.

the kraken, wide wide open
will swallow the souls of a hundred men
and still not be satiated.
there is a need need need
   need.
for that one person.

one hundred other men will leave you starving.

   one does not equal another

honestly,
i saw you had one foot out the door
and baby, i'm not religious
but i swear i screamed so many hail marys
the rosary beads couldn't even keep count.
don't you fucking go.

not you too.

hate is a vengeful apple.
i took bite
          after bite,
only to find that the poison
wasn't rooted in the seeded core.
it was in that venomous intent

          when i opened my mouth in the first place.

i want not
to be perpetually under this yellow light.
rigid,
somewhere between racing, acceleration,
or a hard stop.
love me or love me not:

all i see in yellow is a flat line.

you once gave me butterfly kisses in the lining of my
stomach.
now i stay up late watching the moths.
how they fly with reckless abandon to the light that
sets their heart on fire,
silver
lining the wings that propel them
to their fate.
          holding nothing back.
i'd rather associate the moths and all their honesty
to love,
rather than the deceptive butterflies.
round, loving eyes
are nothing more than elaborate patterns
painted on wings that fly away
faster than every plummeting hope i have left.

    fly away home

what do you call a woman
who raises your son with you
and sleeps in your bed whenever you desire?
who you cast out at the first quivering sign of
adversity?

    a convenience

what do you call a man
who bends to every whim of a woman who left him
ages ago
even if it means destroying the one he 'loves' ?

   a coward

you'll find me
like a werewolf singing to a broken moon.
screaming for what i need,

receiving fragments in return.

it is so sad
that i will not get to write of the tenderness and love.
there was so, so much of it;
laughter gilded the walls of your apartment.
but the way in which you cut it off,
tied a line of fishing wire so tight around the jugular--
it's the detail that hid the tenderness far,
far from here.

you rewrote the story before i could tell it

a man and his whittling knife:
pare me down;
i sleep in the shavings.
the sharper and more powerful i look to you,

the smaller i become

the way you told me you wanted all of me,
with all the strings attached--

i was delighted.

i wouldn't have let you take me if i knew
that you simply meant as a marionette.
i don't belong on a shelf
or under someone's hand.
your manipulative wordplay
bores me.

yawn

not all marionettes are manipulated from the outside;

we all have heartstrings.

you didn't let me say goodbye to the child i helped
raise (for three years)
you kicked me out (the day after moving me in)
you watched in silence as i was harassed (harassed
because i loved you)
you did not treat me as an equal (you took my
autonomy)
you bent to your ex's will (and did not stand up for
me)
you are a bizarre mix of cruelty (and complacency)
you drank straight from the reservoir of my
compassion (and my soft water love)

(you left me dry as a dead thing).

if the truth was a sword,
he sheathed it after its most brutal massacre,
hoping none would see.

however,
nothing can hide the blood.

still warm on your hands.

i loathe you.

    and we aren't even in vegas anymore.

i think i now understand
why the innermost,
most ancient part of our mentality
is called the reptilian brain:

the way it can store old trauma,
and keep polishing it up
to present as brand new again.

cold blooded

i let the bath waters baptize me in their own way,
under my own hand,
in the holy church of my bathroom after a breakup.
i don't know if the guided meditation is working,
or if the lemon softly diffusing into the air is
cleansing,
or if my tea pot nightlight is just a cry to the old times
when my biggest heartbreaks were…
i don't know what. not this.
never this.
the unimaginable future of it isn't him.
of he chose this.
i don't know if i'm sweating from this sweltering
hellfire of reality
or from the water than i ran too hot.
the delicate lemon makes its way through the air,
and i find it smells sweet.
i want it to tell me to be bitter.
to be cold.
but the bathwater is warm
and the lemon,

    the lemon smells so damn sweet.

the wind is drying my sea hair
as i sip a pilsner under the
hot atlantic sun.
i think i will be okay
without your
tepid
pacific
love.

lukewarm

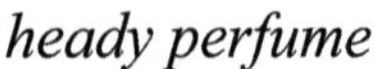

heady perfume

blood, perfume and liquid bone
permeate the air of her earthly den.
it is dark. warm.
amber mist seeps from the lanterns,
encircles the door.
anyone who has said i'm not a woodland thing
is both wrong and right.
too ethereal to be of this plane,
yet burrowed into the mantle;
slumber in the roots. this satin home.
it is from the deep soil that all life bursts.
from the rot we are granted gold.

compress the carbon

one day i'm going to have a large clawfoot bathtub. it
will have a curved copper faucet
and the water will run hot. the steam inside will melt
my crystals and match the mist on the other side of
the glass. the forest will be cold and damp and
mystical. the animals will know me by name; the
town will know me by reputation. the green witch,
the straw-haired eccentric.
the birds will know me from above and from window
sills. they drop bunches of perfumed lilac on the
mantle. the home will pulse with magic, with serenity,
with love. the soil will be soft underfoot, and the
apples will grow gallant in the vale.
all my great grandmothers sit outside in the soft moss,
watching and waiting for me. they don't let the
unsavoury approach.
the hearth is mine, and the heart is full.

care to know your future?

the woods will pull the poems right out of you.
the branches scrape and scream;
slither softly around the chest
and tug.
a gentle reminder at first,
to come home,
          to let the forest beckon.
a tug becomes an anxious pull,
the ribs begin to creak like old cedar. like home.
the highest intensity brings the awe
when ribs split,
the trees reach deeper.
the heart beats in a wooded home
where peace and nature's great fury
dance the waltz among the walls,
and lay the welcome mat just beyond.

come outside

the vines of my survival are reckless.
they wrap around the trellis of all the evil,
of all all the beastly carnations of my sadness,
drinking from my life stream.
the vines of my survival toil with the trellis,
deem it weak,
and crawl into the forest, seeking stronger wilderness.
it is there that they find me,
stirring in a clearing of my own making.
it is here that they find me,
knee deep in the dirt,
waist deep in the moonlight,
awaiting their arrival.
the vines of my survival are reckless.
they wrap themselves around the spine
of the only one with the backbone
to carry them.

they never let go

the child is whimsical, the child is small,
hiding her secrets behind curtain fall.

how all creatives start

there's always been a primal pull
to look upwards at the moon.
the artists stare at her every night. seek solace,
some inexplicable compass in the dark.
something so familiar,
yet so far-off.
she has another face,
one that none of our ghosts have seen
in this human experience.
another face that stares out,
into the rest of the unknown.
she learns it as we do the big dipper,
the north star.
with wonder. with certainty.
with no knowledge at all.
and i wonder,
why is it that we call it
the dark side of the moon,
when she is the side
that gazes off
into eternities of endless light?

the infinity

i long to
feel the pull between my shoulder blades
as my chest opens.
the curiosity of a child.
the art of not knowing.

the nature of accepting

i survived the worst thing that has ever happened to
me.

i can't wait to see what comes next.

my home became salem in 1692;
i, the witch.
i cursed the place, walked out the door,

    and never went back.

i haven't stopped growing since

i dance in the sick, purple liquid. it comes alive, licks my ankles,
poisons my pores. sashay through the venom. the trees are so high;
the sky is absolutely tripping.
the mushroom clouds remind me not of violence.
what a lucky, lucky girl. have the lilacs always sheltered you?

afterglow

about the author

alannah radburn happily lives in canada, a country
she adores for its oceans, mountains and respect for
LGBTQ+ rights. in addition to the 'nature of love'
trilogy, she has had poems published in the literary
magazines 'The First Line' and 'Nightingale &
Sparrow'. alannah loves green tea, vinyl records, and
alaska, her guinea pig.

www.ingramcontent.com/pod-product-compliance
Lightning Source LLC
Chambersburg PA
CBHW051441150726
48000CB00005B/2196